For Mom and Cora, thanks for visiting
the Lowell Observatory with me —S. M.

To my dear friends, Mikey, Natasha, and Geo —S. L.

For my Earthly fans, including Clyde Tombaugh,
Venetia Burney Phair, and Neil deGrasse Tyson —P.

Henry Holt and Company, *Publishers since 1866*
Henry Holt® is a registered trademark of Macmillan Publishing Group, LLC
120 Broadway, New York, NY 10271 • mackids.com

Text copyright © 2023 by Stacy McAnulty
Illustrations copyright © 2023 by Stevie Lewis
All rights reserved.

Our books may be purchased in bulk for promotional, educational, or business use.
Please contact your local bookseller or the Macmillan Corporate and Premium Sales Department
at (800) 221-7945 ext. 5442 or by email at MacmillanSpecialMarkets@macmillan.com.

Library of Congress Cataloging-in-Publication Data is available.
ISBN 978-1-250-81346-6

First edition, 2023
Design by Cindy De la Cruz and Naomi Silverio
The artist used colored pencils and digital tools to create the illustrations for this book.
Printed in China by RR Donnelley Asia Printing Solutions Ltd., Dongguan City, Guangdong Province

1 3 5 7 9 10 8 6 4 2

OUR UNIVERSE

PLUTO!

NOT A PLANET? NOT A PROBLEM!

BY **PLUTO** (WITH **STACY McANULTY**)

ILLUSTRATED BY **PLUTO** (AND **STEVIE LEWIS**)

Henry Holt and Company ✳ New York

Nice to meet you.

The name is PLUTO.
And I'm a proud, playful, and popular non-planet.

Think of me like a lovable family pet.

Think of me like a loyal friend.

Just don't think of me as a boring ole planet.

Planet schmanet, I say.

Our solar system has eight planets.

MERCURY—
the fast one

VENUS—the hot one

MARS—the red one

EARTH—the one with ice cream and books

JUPITER—the big one

Saturn—
the one known for his rings

Neptune—the last one

Uranus—
the sideways one

And then there's me—
the tiny, adorable one, but I'm
not a planet. We were all born
more than 4.5 billion years ago.

We're basically from the same litter.

I'm **special**—
the runt.

ME! Smaller than Mercury.
Even smaller than Earth's Moon.

Mercury = 3,032 miles across

Moon = 2,159 miles across

Pluto = 1,476 miles across

Like Earth,
Mars, and the others,
I spin about my center.

1 Pluto day = 6.4 Earth days

But I also spin *with* Charon, my largest moon. We're playmates, circling each other.

At least four other moons are part of my pack, too.

Styx and Nix.

Kerberos and Hydra.

I'm a poky little non-planet, taking 248 Earth years
to trot around Sun.

And my orbit is unique and not very planet-like.
It's tilted.

I'm round—
a very popular and fetching
look in our solar system.

And check this out! I have a heart.
This spot is called the Tombaugh Regio.

It's a humongous area of flat ice surrounded by mountains of ice. I'm frozen but friendly.

My average temperature is −387°F.

To find me, you have to back up.
Back waaaay up.

If Earth were one step
away from Sun,

I'd be 39 steps
away from Sun.

Ancient Earthlings gazed at the night skies
but could never spot me, no matter how much
I howled or yelped.

Mercury, Venus, Mars, Jupiter, and Saturn can be seen with the naked eye. That means an eye without a telescope—and an eye without underwear.

And then . . .

More than **240 years** ago
(in 1781, to be exact), humans used
a telescope to discover Uranus.

And **65 years** later
(in 1846, to be exact),
they glimpsed Neptune.

I had to wait and wait and wait.
I was getting dog-tired.

Until . . .

Best. Day. Ever!
February 18, 1930

YEARS OF SEARCH ADD NEW PLANET TO SOLAR SYSTEM

FLAGSTAFF, AZ

Cutest Planet Discovered!!!!!

I was no longer a stray.

Talk about puppy love. Earthlings adored me! They declared me the ninth planet.

An eleven-year-old girl from England suggested my name.

I was doggone excited to be added
to the family portrait.

ME →

Over the years, humans set out to know me better.
They used telescopes in space to snap pictures.

Hello, *Hubble!*
Oh, that's a good one.

And, eventually, they sent a spacecraft to do a flyby. It took 9.5 years to reach me.

Hello, NEW HORIZONS! Oh, that's a really good one!

Scientists needed 76 years to realize
I wasn't like the original eight planets.
They made official rules.

A Planet Must:

- ☑ Orbit Sun
- ☑ Be round
- ☐ Clear the neighborhood

Clear the neighborhood: This means being big enough to scare away all other objects in my path around Sun. But I'm too friendly and don't mind sharing my space.

Astronomers came up with a new breed

Dwarf Planet!

And I wasn't alone. Eris and Ceres were named dwarf planets, too.

Years later, Makemake and Haumea joined us.
Someday, I bet there will be even more of us non-planets.

So, remember, the name is Pluto.

I'm not a planet, and that's not a problem.

Dear Pluto Fan,

Are you on Team Planet or Team Dwarf Planet? Personally, I think we should all just be on Team Pluto. It doesn't matter how us Earthlings label him; perky little Pluto is a fascinating part of our solar system.

Isn't it awesome that we have learned so much about our universe that we need to debate and change definitions? Just 100 years ago, humans did not know Pluto existed. Since then, we've found exoplanets, black holes, new moons, the Kuiper Belt, and more. So, let's keep debating how to categorize new discoveries because that means we're making new discoveries. *Yippee!*

Sincerely,

Stacy McAnulty

Author and proud member of Team Pluto

P.S. Light speed is 186,000 miles per second. Science doesn't literally work at light speed, but sometimes it feels like it does. I make every attempt to bring you accurate and up-to-date information, but some material may have changed as our knowledge of the universe has expanded.

Pluto or Earth or Both?

Who can claim the following statements?

1. **"No doubt about it, I'm a planet!"**

EARTH. But Pluto could have made this comment before 2006. That's when the International Astronomical Union (IAU) created official rules for planetary status. They also set up a new category called dwarf planets, and Pluto was a founding member.

2. **"Woof! Woof! I share a name with a famous cartoon dog."**

PLUTO. In spring 1930, the (former) planet's name was suggested by Venetia Burney, an eleven-year-old girl from England. Around the same time, the Walt Disney Company had a character called Rover, a pet dog owned by Minnie Mouse. In 1931, the dog was renamed Pluto and became Mickey's pet.

3. **"Looking for mountains? Then look at me!"**

BOTH. Earth, of course, has plenty of mountains, and some are even in the oceans. The mountains on Pluto are made of water-ice. Pluto is so cold that ice is harder than rock.

4. **"Zoooooom! I spin faster than Mercury."**

BOTH. It takes Earth 24 hours—or, as we call it, one day—to do one full spin on her axis. Pluto needs 6.4 Earth days to complete a spin. But both Earth and Pluto are much faster than Mercury, who requires 59 Earth days to complete one spin on his axis.

5. **"Patience, people! Sunlight takes five and a half hours to reach me."**

PLUTO. On average, our favorite dwarf planet is 3.7 billion miles away from Sun, and it takes sunlight 5.5 hours to make that trip. Sunlight only needs eight minutes to reach Earth.

6. **"Double trouble? Dynamic duo? Because of my big moon, I'm often called a double-body system."**

PLUTO. Our Moon revolves around Earth. Pluto's largest moon, Charon, does not orbit Pluto. Instead, they are closer in size than Earth and Moon, Pluto and Charon circle each other, making them a double-body system.

Pluto by the Numbers

9—For 75 years, Pluto was considered the ninth planet from Sun.

3,700,000,000—The average distance between Sun and Pluto is 3.7 billion miles.

39—The distance between Earth and Sun is 1 astronomical unit (AU). The distance between Pluto and Sun is 39 AUs.

153—A day on Pluto is 153 hours long. That's more than six Earth days.

248—A Plutonian year is 248 Earth years long. Since Pluto was discovered, it has yet to complete a lap around Sun.

1,476—Pluto's diameter is 1,476 miles, which is smaller than Moon's diameter and about half the width of the contiguous United States.

5—Astronomers have observed five moons orbiting Pluto: Charon, Styx, Nix, Kerberos, and Hydra.

1930—Clyde Tombaugh discovered Pluto on February 18, 1930, at the Lowell Observatory in Arizona.

What's a Planet?

At the 2006 IAU conference, astronomers crowned Pluto a dwarf planet. Some people called this a demotion, but let's simply think of it as a change. You see, in the years leading up to this change, scientists were discovering new objects in the farthest parts of our solar system. All these new finds were much smaller than Pluto, until Eris was spotted. Scientists had to decide if Eris should be considered a planet, too. It was time for a good definition of a planet, with clear rules.

Planet
- Orbits Sun
- Is round
- Clears its neighborhood

The first two requirements are easy to understand. Planets revolve around Sun. Earth does this in 365 days, and we call it a year. Planets are generally round. But "clears its neighborhood" is harder to understand, and this is where Pluto fails to meet the mark. (Same for Eris.)

Imagine Earth, the other seven planets, and Pluto circling Sun like they're on a racetrack, each in its own lane. Planets will keep their lanes clear of any other objects of similar size. Not so for Pluto, who is part of the crowded Kuiper Belt. Pluto has not cleared his neighborhood. He shares his orbit and is, therefore, not a planet. He's a friendly dwarf planet.

Dwarf Planet
- Orbits Sun
- Is round
- Does **not** clear its neighborhood
- Is not a satellite (meaning: not a moon)

Sources

Cain, Fraser. "Who Was Pluto Named After?" *Universe Today*. April 26, 2008. universetoday.com/13900/who-was-pluto-named-after/.

Choi, Charles Q. "The Mountains on Pluto Have Super Weird Methane Ice Snowcaps." Space.com. October 13, 2020. space.com/pluto-mountains-methane-snow caps-form-reverse.html.

D23. "10 Things You Didn't Know About Walt Disney's Pluto." Accessed February 9, 2022. d23.com/10-things-you-didnt-know-about-walt-disneys-pluto/.

International Astronomical Union. "Pluto and the Developing Landscape of Our Solar System." IAU.org. Accessed February 9, 2022. iau.org/public/themes/pluto/.

Kaplan, Karen. "Two for the Price of One: The Unique Binary System of Pluto and Charon." *Los Angeles Times*. July 15, 2015. latimes.com/science/sciencenow/la-sci -sn-pluto-charon-binary-system-new-horizons-20150714-htmlstory.html.

NASA JPL. "What Is a Dwarf Planet?" Jet Propulsion Laboratory California Institute of Technology. May 12, 2015. jpl.nasa.gov/videos/what-is-a-dwarf-planet.

NASA Science. "Planets: Overview." Solar System Exploration. Accessed February 9, 2022. solarsystem.nasa.gov/planets/overview/.

NASA Science. "Pluto: Overview." Solar System Exploration. Accessed February 9, 2022. solarsystem.nasa.gov/planets/dwarf-planets/pluto/overview/.

Overbye, Dennis. "Pluto Is Demoted to 'Dwarf Planet.'" *New York Times*. August 24, 2006. nytimes.com/2006/08/24/science/space/25pluto.html.

Owen, Tobias Chant. "Pluto." *Encyclopedia Britannica*. Accessed February 9, 2022. britannica.com/place/Pluto-dwarf-planet.